HUE COLORING

Trust in God:Inspirational Quotes from the Bible
An Adult Coloring Book

ISBN-13: 978-1533517227
ISBN-10: 1533517223
Copyright © 2015 Hue Coloring

IN THIS COLORING BOOK...

50 Inspiriational Coloring Quote designs are included in this adult coloring book to help you relax and make your life more colorful. These illustrations are created for you to bring enjoyment to your life, and designed with beautiful patterns that appeal to adult eyes.

TIPS TO A FUN COLORING

Find a quiet space. It's easier to focus on what you are doing when there are no distractions.

Organize your materials. Lay out your coloring book and crayons, pens, or pencils.

Set the mood. Turn on some tranquil music, diffuse lavender or another relaxing oil, and make sure you have your preferred drink at hand.

Select your picture. Which image speaks to you today? That's the one you should color. Choose your palette. Select the colors you will be using for your image.

Begin coloring. This is the fun part. Don't worry about getting everything perfect; just start. If you feel you don't want to do it anymore, just stop!

SHOW US YOUR CREATION!

We'd love to hear from you, show us what you created.
Facebook: www.facebook.com/huecoloring
Pinterest: www.pinterest.com/huecoloring

Please be sure to subscribe to our newsletter by visiting: huecoloring.com. We'll show you our latest coloring projects as well as giving you information of the best deals.

Set your minds on things above, Not on earthly things. Colossians 3:2

Look to the LORD and his strength;
seek his face always.

1 CHRONICLES 16:11

Do to others as you would have them do to you.

Luke 6:31

You are the light
of the world.
A town built
on a hill
cannot be hidden.

Matthew 5:14

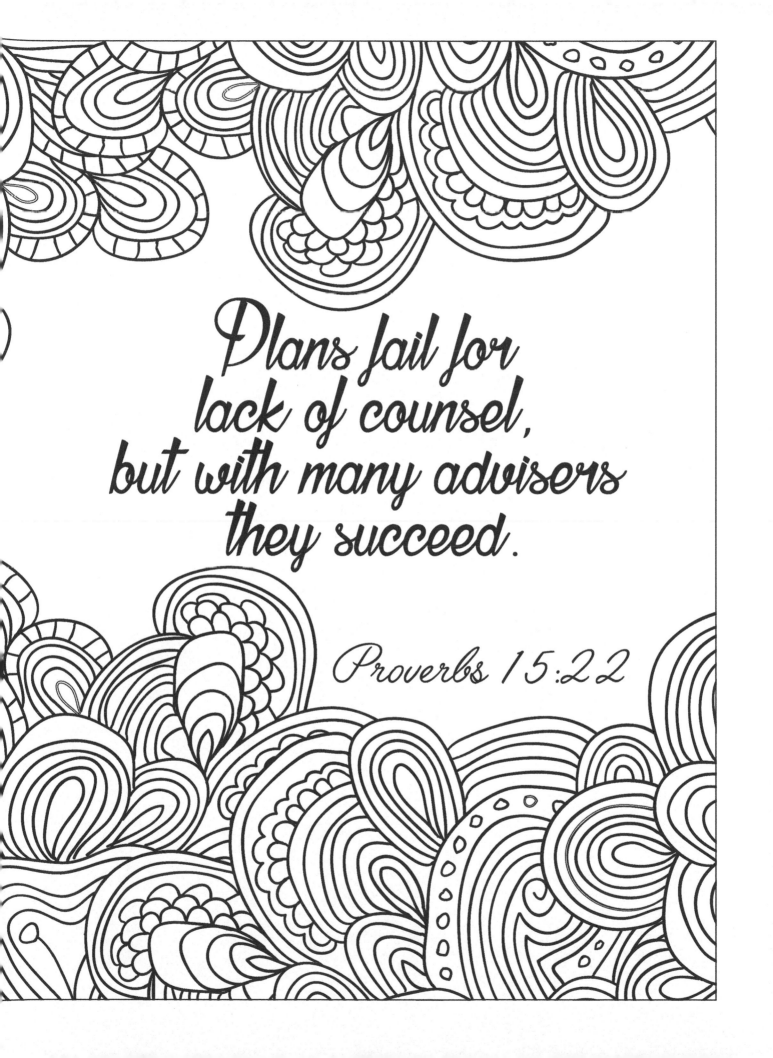

Plans fail for lack of counsel, but with many advisers they succeed.

Proverbs 15:22

Proverbs 18:10

The name of the
LORD
is a
fortified tower;
the righteous run
to it
and
are safe.

My son, if your heart is wise,
then my heart will be glad indeed

PROVERBS 23:15

As iron sharpens iron, so one person sharpens another.

PROVERBS 27:17

Be joyful in hope, patient in affliction, faithful in prayer.

Romans 12:12

THE
LORD
HAS DONE
it this very day;
LET US REJOICE TODAY
AND
BE GLAD.

PSALM 118:24

But Godliness with contentment is great gain.

1 Timothy 6:6

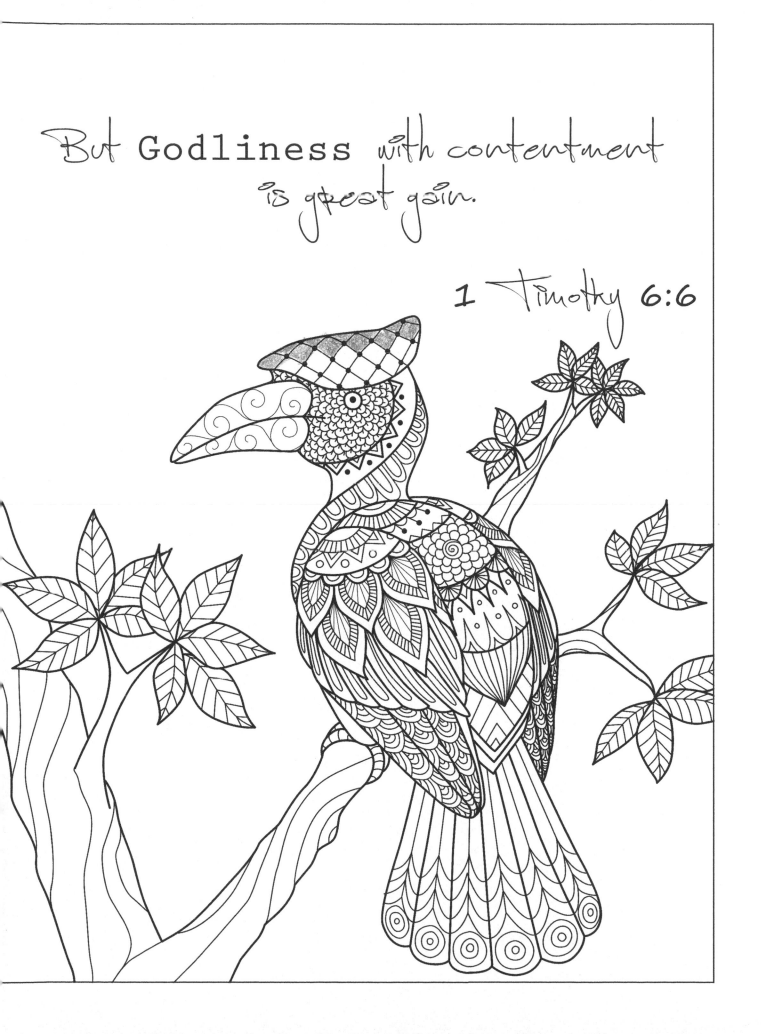

because he **loves** our nation and has built our synagogue

Luke 7:5

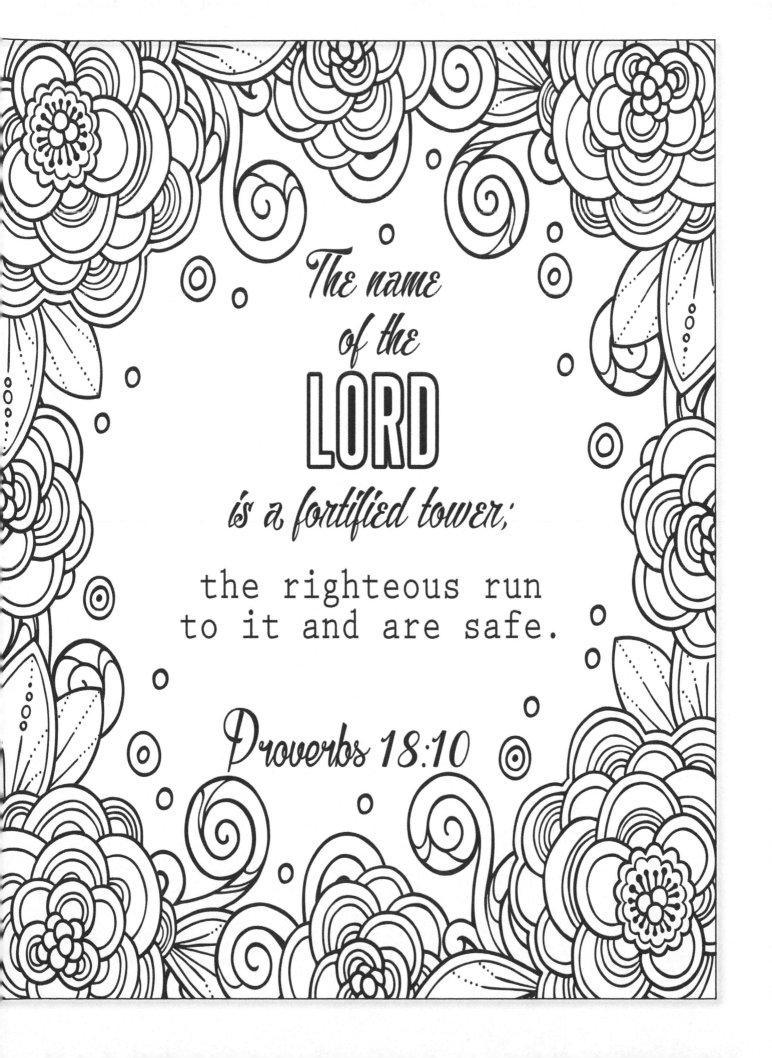

The name
of the
LORD
is a fortified tower;

the righteous run
to it and are safe.

Proverbs 18:10

For the Spirit God gave us does not make us timid, but gives us power, love and self-discipline.

2 Timothy 1:7

I keep my eyes always on the LORD. With him at my right hand, I will not be shaken.

psalm 16:8

Cast your cares on the

LORd

and he will sustain you;

he will never let the righteous be shaken.

Psalm 55:22

You will keep in perfect peace
those whose minds are steadfast,
because they trust in you.

Isaiah 26:3

I am laid low in the dust;
preserve my life according to your word.

PSALM 119:25

Hope deferred
makes the heart sick,
but a longing fulfilled
is a tree of life.
Proverbs 13:12

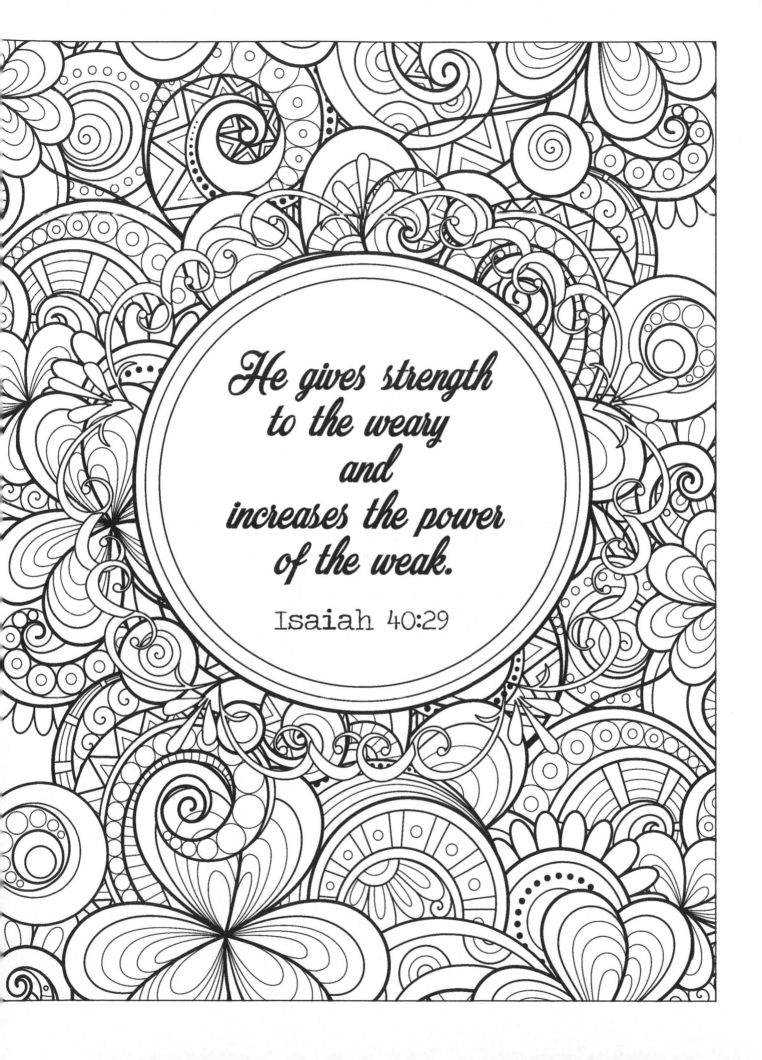

He gives strength
to the weary
and
increases the power
of the weak.

Isaiah 40:29

SHOW US YOUR CREATION!

We'd love to hear from you, show us what you created.
Facebook: www.facebook.com/huecoloring
Pinterest: www.pinterest.com/huecoloring

Please be sure to subscribe to our newsletter by visiting:
huecoloring.com. We'll show you our latest coloring projects
as well as giving you information of the best deals.

Made in the USA
Las Vegas, NV
02 December 2020

11862293R00059